Little SantOs

"Overcomes Obstacles"

SantOs vallejo

Print information available on the last page

Rev. date: 03/17/2016

To order additional copies of this book, contact:
Xlibris
1-888-795-4274
www.Xlibris.com
Orders@Xlibris.com

Little Santos is a great firefighter who loves his job. Waking up and putting on the firefighter uniform is one of the joys of his life. The past three years as a firefighter has been awesome, but Little Santos was unaware that things were about to change.

Today was going to be different. As he walked up to the fire station doors, his heart started beating faster. He was eager to open those doors and walk in.

Little Santos was excited because he was about to begin working with a new group of firefighters. He remembered how it felt his first day on the job three years ago. His anticipation of starting a new shift was thrilling. Since he loved his job so much, he knew he would fit right in.

All the firefighters greeted Little Santos every time they saw him. All but one. His name was **Bruce**, but everyone knew him as **"The Beast"**. **"Bruce the Beast"**, they would say. He would constantly question Little Santos. He always made him feel small. "What's your weakest area as a firefighter?" **Bruce** would ask.

Little Santos felt very intimidated. "I'm not sure sir." Little Santos would humbly reply.

The first day on the job with the new shift was going great. At about 6 o'clock in the evening the firefighters began working on different tasks.

Little Santos started to clean and shine his boots. One firefighter was washing dishes. He was one of the drivers of the fire trucks. Little Santos then hears someone walk in. It was **Bruce**. He walked up to Little Santos and stood behind him. He said, "The driver will not wash his own dishes, you will wash them for him!" Little Santos knew it was not right for **Bruce** to order him to do that, but he didn't want a conflict with **Bruce**.

Little Santos started to wash the dishes. **Bruce** stood behind him with his arms crossed to intimidate him and to make sure he did it right. **Bruce the Beast** said, "You're going to have to prove yourself to be a firefighter here!"

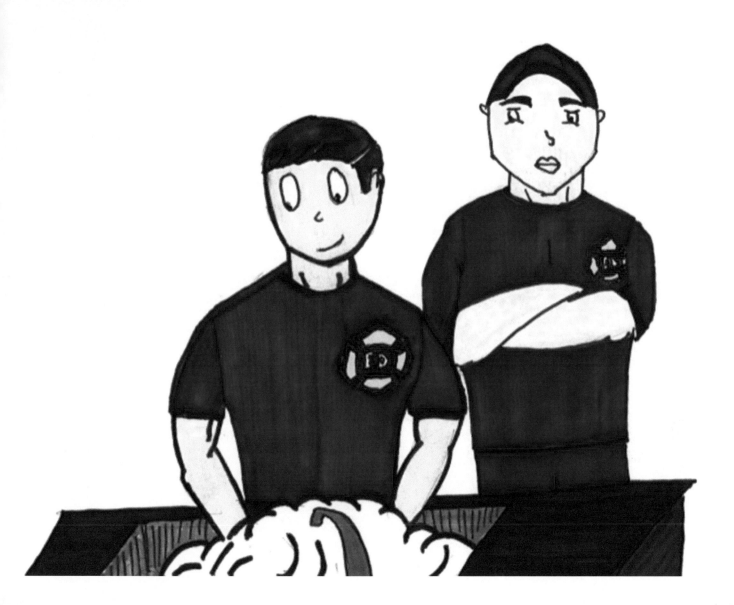

Little Santos felt discouraged and started to doubt himself and his skills as a firefighter. He began questioning himself, "Why did I go into this field of work?" "Why would God place me in a place where I was not wanted?" "What can I do to show **Bruce** that I am a firefighter just like him?"

Little Santos was feeling so discouraged and alone. He didn't know who to turn to for help. A wise person once told him to find someone to talk to when you're feeling down. Little Santos did just that.

He reached out to Gilbert, a firefighter friend, who had been working with him for the past three years. Gilbert advised him that everything would be okay. He reminded him that God had great plans for his life. Gilbert was a great friend to Little Santos.

All the firefighters started noticing how **Bruce the Beast** was treating Little Santos. The lieutenant heard the firefighters talking about the bullying. The lieutenant decided to talk to Little Santos about the situation.

He asked Little Santos if he wanted him to speak to **Bruce**. Little Santos said, "No." The lieutenant then asked, "Do you want to be moved to another shift or another station?" Little Santos again said, "No." Little Santos believed in conflict resolution. He knew that God would never put him in a situation he couldn't handle.

That evening, Little Santos suited up in full gear and walked out of the station to be alone. He looked up to the sky and began to pray.

"God, do I belong here?" Little Santos paused. "Please show me what I can do differently and give me the wisdom to know what choices to make."

Little Santos was desperate to resolve this problem because he didn't know how much more he could take.

Little Santos knew he had to change his way of thinking. For the next few weeks, Little Santos was gaining his confidence as a firefighter again because he knew God was with him. Every time the fire alarm would go off at the station, he was ready to fulfill his duties. He knew people were counting on him to save them.

When you're a firefighter, you never know when an emergency call will come in.

One early morning, the firefighters awoke to a fire alarm. They all got up and jumped into action. It was their first call of the day.

The firefighters were told it was a car accident and a child was injured. When they arrived at the scene, Little Santos realized the child needed treatment, but was being uncooperative with the first responders. Little Santos knew he had to convince the child to accept help. The child listened to Little Santos. Little Santos was then able to carry him to safety.

The second call of the day came in around noon. The firefighters were told it was an elderly lady that had fallen in her home and couldn't get up. When the firefighters arrived on the scene, the only way into her home was through a very small window.

The only firefighter able to fit through the very small window was Little Santos. He was the perfect size. He climbed up the ladder and crawled in the window. Little Santos reached the elderly lady just in time. He helped her up and out the front door to a waiting ambulance. The elderly lady didn't think anyone could have fit through the tiny window. She thanked Little Santos for his bravery.

The last call of the day happened in the late evening hours. It was a type of call that no firefighter wants to receive…a "man down" call. Little Santos was the first one off the fire truck. He rushed to a man lying on the floor. The ambulance arrived and placed the man on a gurney. Little Santos performed CPR to help keep the man alive.

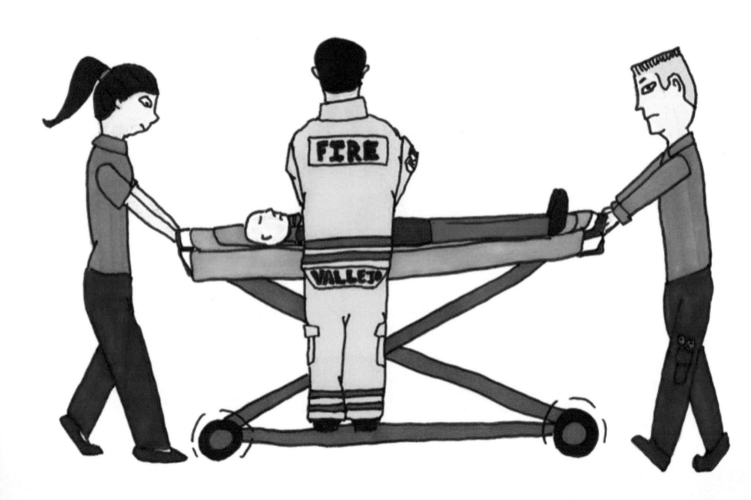

As the ambulance drove off to take the man to the hospital, Little Santos felt fulfilled. He knew he had done his best!

On the drive back to the fire station, Little Santos was thinking about everything that happened. He knew being a firefighter was what he wanted to be for the rest of his life. Saving lives and fighting fires made him happy.

The following day, the lieutenant told Little Santos that the son of the man he helped rescue wanted to thank him for saving his dad. The visit from the young man brought joy to Little Santos.

Little Santos then received a commendation from his lieutenant for helping save a man's life. ✝

Little Santos was given a medal of honor for his bravery and quick action in saving lives. He gained the respect of all his firefighter friends. Although, Little Santos was still little, everyone now saw him as a big man. A big man of courage, strength and dedication to his job.

Firefighters must stay fit in order to be physically able to perform their duties. When Little Santos was lifting weights one day, **Bruce** approached him wanting to talk. He apologized for his rude behavior. He realized he had been treating him badly and was ashamed. Little Santos was quick to forgive **Bruce**. They talked, laughed and helped each other lift weights. They became friends that day and **Bruce** was no longer known as **Bruce the Beast** anymore. His name was just **Bruce**.

Always do your best.

Always try to make friends.

The End